Celebrate! Harvest

Polly Goodman

an imprint of Hodder
Children's Books

Celebrate!

CHINESE NEW YEAR

CHRISTMAS

DIWALI

EASTER

ID-UL-FITR

PASSOVER

This book is based on the original title **Harvest** in the **Festivals** series, published in 1997 by Wayland Publishers Ltd.

Text copyright © 2000 Hodder Wayland
Volume copyright © 2000 Hodder Wayland

Series concept: Polly Goodman

Published in Great Britain in 2000 by Hodder Wayland, an imprint of Hodder Children's Books.

A Catalogue record for this book is available from the British Library.

ISBN 0 7502 2824 5

Printed and bound in Italy byEurografica S.p.a.

Hodder Children's Books
A division of Hodder Headline Ltd
338 Euston Road, London NW1 3BH

Picture credits
The Bridgeman Art Library 9 both; Britstock 20; C.M Dixon 11 both; Chris Fairclough Colour Library cover (bottom), 4 (top left), 6 bottom, 17 top; ET Archive 14; Mary Evans 8/9, 10; Eye Ubiquitous 4 bottom right, cover and 13 top (Paul Seheult), 19 top; Hutchison 25, 28 bottom; Images cover (middle, top and left); Impact title page (Mark Henley), 5 top left (Christophe Bluntzer), 7 (Mark Henley), 18 (Francesco Rizzoli), 23 (Christophe Bluntzer), 24 top (Piers Cavendish), 27 top (Piers Cavendish); Japan National Tourist Organization 22; Christine Osborne 17 bottom, 29; Oxford Picture Library 27 bottom; Panos 4 bottom left, 24 bottom; Tony Stone Worldwide 5 top (David Young Wolff), 15 (David Young Wolff), 26/7 (Simon Jauncey); Topham 5 bottom left; Trip 19 bottom, 21; Hodder Wayland Picture Library 12, 13; Zefa 16.

Contents

Harvest around the World

▲ In Britain, these schoolchildren are sitting in front of a harvest display.

▲ In Nigeria, the fishing festival celebrates the start of the fishing season.

▲ Women in India decorate the ground for the festival of Pongal.

▲ In the USA, people remember the Pilgrim Fathers' first successful harvest at Thanksgiving.

▲ At the Mid-Autumn festival in China, people eat moon cakes and pray for a good rice harvest.

◀ New Zealand is in the southern hemisphere, so harvest festivals are in February and March.

A Good Harvest

Every day of the year, a crop is gathered somewhere in the world. For centuries, people have held festivals to celebrate a good harvest.

◄ In Europe, grapes are harvested in November.

There are many different harvest festivals and they take place throughout the year.

Some festivals celebrate crops such as rice or corn. Others celebrate animals such as cows.

All harvest festivals are happy times of giving thanks and sharing.

A World of Harvests

Harvest festivals take place at different times of year depending on the crop they celebrate and the country in which they take place.

In New Zealand, the corn harvest is in February or March. In Europe, it is between August and October.

▲ A plantain harvest in southern India.

Harvest in the Past

In the past, in many countries, farming was much harder than it is today. There were no tractors or combine harvesters, so everything was done by hand. Everyone helped at harvest-time.

This engraving ▶ shows Chinese people in the nineteenth century praying to the moon for a good harvest.

8

◄ This painting shows people in the sixteenth century making hay.

After weeks of back-breaking work, people celebrated the harvest with feasts and parties.

Some people held special ceremonies. They hoped these would help produce a good crop the next year.

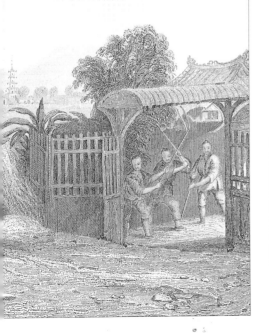

◄ People using scythes to cut wheat.

Corn dollies

In some parts of the world, people believed a spirit lived in the crops. At harvest-time, they thought the spirit was hiding in the last bundle of stalks.

They made the last bundle into a corn dollie to hold the spirit from one harvest to the next.

▲ A traditional corn dollie.

Human Sacrifice

Hundreds of years ago, people in Ecuador, South America, sacrificed 100 children every year at harvest, to help their crops the following year.

Greek myth

In ancient Greece, Demeter was the goddess of the harvest.

There is a story about her daughter, Persephone, who was kidnapped by the King of the Underworld.

Demeter was so angry that she made all the crops fail and there was a terrible famine.

Eventually, Persephone was allowed back on earth for nine months every year.

▲ A painting showing Persephone and the King of the Underworld.

◄ This tomb painting shows the Italian corn goddess Ceres, with two helpers. Can you see the corn she is holding?

Religious Festivals

Christian harvest festivals

For Christians, sharing is an important part of harvest festivals.

All over the world, in the autumn, Christians take gifts of food to their church. The gifts make a colourful display for a special church service.

Some gifts are food people have grown themselves. Other gifts are bought in a shop. It doesn't matter where the food comes from. The important part of the ceremony is the giving.

After the service, the food is given to the homeless and other people in need.

◀ Children in Britain celebrating the harvest festival at school.

This loaf of bread has been baked ▶ in the shape of a sheaf of corn for a harvest display.

Tithes

In Britain in the past, farmers had to give a tenth of their harvest every year to the Church.

Every tenth pig or lamb had to be given to the vicar, and every tenth sheaf of corn went to his tithe barn.

The farmers hated this system and always tried to find ways of not paying.

▲ In London, market traders dress up in pearl buttons for a festival at harvest time.

Thanksgiving

At Thanksgiving, Americans celebrate the first successful harvest of the Pilgrim Fathers.

The Pilgrim Fathers were the first Europeans to make their home in North America. They arrived on a ship called the *Mayflower*.

Their first winter, the pilgrims had no food and many starved to death. Local Native Americans helped them, and by the end of the next summer, they had a good harvest. The pilgrims held a great feast with the Native Americans to celebrate.

◄ Pilgrim Fathers in black clothes joining the *Mayflower* before it sailed for North America.

Today, American families celebrate Thanksgiving with a special meal.

They remember the Pilgrim Fathers and the Native Americans who helped them with their first harvest.

The Thanksgiving meal usually includes turkey with cranberry sauce, followed by pumpkin pie.

▲ A Thanksgiving meal in the USA.

Holiday

Thanksgiving is now a public holiday in the USA. Everybody has time off work. It is held on the fourth Thursday of November each year.

Shavuot

Shavuot is a Jewish festival which used to be called the Feast of the Harvest. It is held in May or June each year and celebrates giving the first fruits to God in thanks.

◄ Homes and synagogues are decorated with flowers for Shavuot.

Foods for Shavuot

Cheesecake and pancakes filled with cheese are traditional foods for Shavuot.

Sukkot

Sukkot is another Jewish festival.

During the week of Sukkot, Jews remember their ancestors, who travelled through the desert to what is now Israel.

Some people make a shelter and decorate it with greenery for Sukkot. It is called a sukkah.

Every day during Sukkot, four plants are waved in the air. They are symbols of fertility. The plants are citron, palm, myrtle and willow.

▲ These children are decorating a sukkah for Sukkot.

Citrons for sale at Sukkot, ▶ in Jerusalem, Israel.

Pongal

Pongal is a Hindu festival held in southern India. It celebrates the sugar-cane harvest. Pongal lasts for two or three days.

The word pongal means 'boiling'. Rice boiled with sugar is an important food in the festival.

A sweet rice pudding is made and offered to the gods. Then it is eaten in a big feast.

The second day of Pongal is devoted to the sun god, so the rice pudding is offered to the sun.

Cattle Pongal

Cattle are sacred to Hindus. The third day of Pongal is devoted to them. Each family chooses a cow and decorates it. After feeding it with boiled rice, they drive it off to the sound of music.

Women decorating ▶
the ground with
coloured paint
for Pongal.

Onam

Onam is another harvest festival from southern
India. People decorate their homes, wear new
clothes and give presents. After visiting the
temple to give thanks for the harvest, they have a
feast of spicy rice, vegetables and sweet puddings.

After the feast ▶
of Pongal, there are
races in long boats
carved with animals.

Baisakhi

Baisakhi is a Sikh festival. It is held just before the first corn harvest in April.

Baisakhi is also the beginning of the Sikh religious year. It is a fun festival, with games, races and spectacular dancing.

People listen to speeches about the gurus, the Sikh religious teachers.

▲ Sikh men at a fair.

▲ Fruit and nuts for sale at the festival of Mihr Jashan.

Mihr Jashan

Mihr Jashan is a Zoroastrian festival. Zoroastrians live mainly in Iran and northern India and they belong to one of the oldest religions in the world.

At Mihr Jashan in October, Zoroastrians celebrate the harvest with five days of feasts and parties. Gifts of wheat and cotton are taken to the temple.

Other Festivals

Japan

Rice is the most important type of food in Japan, so many festivals began as celebrations of the rice harvest.

In the Lantern Festival, in August, the streets are filled with lanterns hanging from huge bamboo frames. Each lantern represents a grain of rice.

In November, the New Taste Festival celebrates the end of the rice harvest. People feast, dance and drink rice wine.

▲ Each man balances up to forty lanterns at the Lantern Festival in Japan.

China

In China, the Mid-Autumn festival celebrates the full moon. Special cakes are made called moon cakes, with a picture of the moon on top.

Children in Hong Kong ▶ at the Mid-Autumn festival.

At the Mid-Autumn festival, streets and shops are decorated with lanterns, and children are allowed to stay up late eating moon cakes while they watch the full moon rise.

Africa

Africa is so big, there are many different important foods, including maize, cassava, plantain and beans.

Special ceremonies surround the planting and harvesting of certain crops.

In Nigeria, a fishing festival in February celebrates the start of the fishing season. The festival lasts for two days and there are fishing displays, swimming and canoe-racing.

▲ Wheat is harvested in Kenya.

A fishing festival ▶ in Nigeria.

◄ These yams have been collected for the yam festival in Ghana.

Yam festival

In September, the Ashanti people of Ghana hold a yam festival. Yams are eaten in feasts, and there is drumming and dancing.

Kwanza

Kwanza is a festival that was started in 1966 in the USA, to remind black people of their African roots. It begins on 26 December and lasts for seven days. Stories are told, songs are sung and there is a feast at the end of the week.

Harvests Today

Today, most people in wealthy countries do not see their food being harvested. Food is bought from supermarkets and comes from all over the world.

Farm machinery means that few people need to work on the land to grow crops.

But harvest is still a time for giving thanks for our food, and for sharing what we have with others.

Combine harvesters do ▶ the work of hundreds of people.

Pineapple rings are ▶ put in tins in Africa. The tins can be sold in supermarkets all over the world.

◀ Many people today buy all their food in supermarkets. You can find out where it was grown by looking on the packaging.

Calendar of Harvest festivals

January
PONGAL
Pongal is held in southern India and lasts for two or three days.

January
LOHRI
Lohri is held in northern India. It celebrates children born in the past year.

February
FISHING FESTIVAL
A fishing festival is held in Nigeria every February. It celebrates the start of the fishing season.

13 or 14 April
BAISAKHI
Baiskakhi is a Sikh festival just before the first corn harvest. It is also the start of the Sikh year.

May/June
SHAVUOT
Shavuot is a Jewish festival that started as a celebration of harvest.

5–7 August
LANTERN FESTIVAL
The Lantern Festival in northern Japan celebrates the ripening of the rice crop.

August/September
ONAM
Onam is celebrated in Kerala, southern India.

September
YAM FESTIVAL
A yam festival is held in Ghana every September.

28

September
MOON VIEWING
A traditional festival in China and Japan. People gaze at the full moon and pray for a good harvest.

September
MID-AUTUMN FESTIVAL
A similar festival to the Moon Viewing. In China, people make and eat special moon cakes.

September/October
SUKKOT
A Jewish festival that lasts for a week. Special plants are waved in the air to represent fertility.

October in Europe, March in Australia and New Zealand
HARVEST FESTIVAL
Christians take gifts of food to their church.

Fourth Thursday in November in the USA
THANKSGIVING
Thanksgiving celebrates the first successful harvest of the Pilgrim Fathers.

23 November
LABOUR THANKSGIVING DAY
A Japanese national holiday.

26 December to 1 January
KWANZA
A celebration of African culture by African-Americans.

Glossary

ancestors   People far back in someone's family.

crops   Grain, fruit or vegetables grown for food.

fertility   The ability to produce seeds or plants.

myth   Ancient story.

parson   In the past, the parson was the local priest of the Church of England. He took tithes from farmers.

pilgrims   People who make a long journey to a holy place.

sacrifice   When a person or animal is killed to please a god.

scythes   Traditional tools used for cutting cereal crops such as wheat and barley.

sheaf   A bundle of corn that has just been harvested.

southern hemisphere   The half of the world below the Equator.

spirit   An invisible being, such as a ghost.

symbols   Objects that stand for something else.

synagogues   Buildings where Jews pray and learn about their religion.

temples   Buildings in which people pray and worship.

tithes   A payment made by British farmers in the past to the Church. Farmers had to pay a tenth (or a tithe), to their local parson.

Finding Out More

BOOKS TO READ

Celebration! by Barnabas and Anabel Kindersley (Dorling Kindersley, 1997)

Feasts and Festivals by Jacqueline Dineen (Belitha, 1995)

A Feast of Festivals by Hugo Slim (Marshall Pickering, 1996)

Festival Cookbooks series (*Christian Festivals Cookbook, Jewish Festivals Cookbook, Chinese Festivals Cookbook, Hindu Festivals Cookbook*) (Hodder Wayland, 2000)

Festivals of the World series (*Germany, India, Israel and Mexico*) (Heinemann, 1997)

Festivals through the Year series (*Autumn, Spring, Summer, Winter*) (Heinemann, 1998)

Fiesta series (*Brazil, Ireland, Jamaica, Turkey, Vietnam etc*) (Franklin Watts, 1998)

Food and Festivals series (*A Flavour of Brazil, The Caribbean, France, Germany, India, Israel, Japan, Kenya, Mexico, West Africa*) (Hodder Wayland, 1998)

Looking at Christianity: Festivals (Hodder Wayland, 1998)

Looking at Judaism: Festivals (Hodder Wayland, 1998)

Thanksgiving and other Harvest Festivals by Marilyn Miller (Evans, 1996)

What's Special to Me? Religious Food (Wayland, 1998)

The World of Festivals by Philip Steele (Hodder Wayland, 1996)

OTHER RESOURCES

Festivals Worksheets by Albany Bilbe and Liz George (Wayland, 1998)

25 photocopiable, copyright-free worksheets on the topic of festivals.

The Festival Year: an annual calendar of multifaith festivals (Festival Shop).

USEFUL ADDRESSES

The Festival Shop, 56 Poplar Road, Kings Heath, Birmingham B14 7AG

Tel: 0121 444 0444

SHAP Working Party on World Religions and The National Society's RE Centre, 36 Causton Street, London SW1P 4AU Tel: 0207 932 1194

Index